VAPOURS

HAZEL LONGUET

Happy Reading
Longuet

Novel Experience

The events and conversations in this book have been set down to the best of the author's ability, although some names and details have been changed to protect the privacy of individuals.

Copyright © 2018 by Hazel Longuet

All rights reserved. No part of this book may be reproduced or used in any manner without written permission of the copyright owner except for the use of quotations in a book review. For more information, address: hlonguet@hazellonguet.com

A Novel Experience book.
First published in Great Britain in 2018 by Novel Experience
First Print Edition November 2018

Cover design by Hazel Longuet

Edited by Briar Rose Editing
www.briarroseediting.com

www.hazellonguet.com

I dedicate this to the people & animals I have loved and lost. You may be on a different plane now, but I'm sure we'll meet again someday.

Dedicated to the memory of:

Ivy Longuet, Leslie Yandall, Fred Longuet, Ahmed Mahallowy, Laura Bendall, Nermine Shoukry, Magued Gabr, Katy Fox, Michelle

And to the animals waiting for me:

Merli, Asha, Venus, Apollo, Orka, Samba, Rocky, Pablo, Hitler (I explain this name later in the book), Rex, Scraggy, and Janey

FOREWORD

Have you ever wondered what inspires an author to write? What triggers that creative part of their brain to pull a story out of the ether?

What made Charles Dickens write so emotionally about the poor and their struggle to rise from their often lowly birth status?

How did the Bronte sisters, sheltered daughters of a clergyman, dream up such diverse characters as Heathcliff and Jane Eyre?

I can't answer for their muses. However, in this anthology of true stories about my paranormal experiences, I hope to illuminate the driving factors behind my fascination with the supernatural and the following questions:

What comes next?

Can life continue after the body dies?

Is there more to life than science can explain?

Foreword

I have lived a very analytical life working as an international business consultant with some of the world's largest telecommunications companies. By nature, I'm a quiet thinker, and I need to understand and look at the full picture in acute detail before coming to a decision. I will base judgements on facts and figures. Yet, despite this, I've experienced so many bizarre and unexplainable phenomena, I can only conclude that science has still to explore and explain the boundaries of life. I'm sharing my experiences with you today to show why I've come to that conclusion and how it's influenced MY personal muse.

Although I'm only in the early stages of my writing career, I've already outlined my next few stories. Each of them focuses on some form of life after death or the paranormal. Will this always be the case? It's early to say, but I've a niggling suspicion it may be.

Every one of the stories you are about to read happened to me personally. Some are associated with harrowing times in my life, so I've eliminated or changed names where necessary to protect the privacy of the living.

Hazel x

1

THE BLUE BOY

Sometimes I wonder if society teaches us to disconnect from our more spiritually connected selves. As children, we are open to everything around us in a way we can never recreate in later life. But that open portal is closed, bit by bit, with every negative comment an adult makes to a child. How often are children told:

"Don't be so silly. There's nothing there."

"Who are you talking to? Oh... your 'imaginary' friend."

"There's no one here. You're imagining it."

The "reality" of the adult world suppresses our little open souls, and soon our connection withers, much like an under-used muscle. Then, one day, it stops working totally, paralysed by neglect, and we forget that we once had friends and saw people that the adults couldn't.

At around three years old, I had my first experience of

meeting someone that no one else saw. It was a little boy who came to visit me when I was on my own and would scurry away shyly if we heard anyone approaching. I can't tell you his age as I view him via the hazy memories of a young child, but he was older than me, so maybe seven. He would appear, from nowhere, in the bedroom I shared with my sister. We'd sit with our backs to my bed as we whispered and laughed.

It didn't seem odd I only saw him when I was on my own or that a strange boy came into my house. I accepted his presence as normal and enjoyed his company. I don't recall much more except that he dressed a little oddly. His shirt was covered in ruffles that weren't common in 1970s England. I remember him ducking under my bed to hide when adults came, and I'd lean over once they'd gone to give him the all-clear. He was probably my earliest friend, a sweet and soulful boy whose skin was a sickly shade of blue - not a bright Smurf blue but the unhealthy blue of a vein seen through skin.

I chatted to my parents freely about my friend, the little blue boy. My mum has always believed he was a figment of my imagination based on a picture I had in my room of a boy dressed in blue. It seemed logical except for one small flaw - this boy wore dark green knickerbocker trousers and a white ruffled shirt. He didn't wear blue; he *was* blue.

I don't remember when I stopped seeing him. It wasn't a momentous event. He seems to have faded out of my life, but with the benefit of hindsight, I believe I drifted out of his. Adults had slammed my doors shut, insisting he didn't exist. After all, there are no such things as ghosts... are there?

2

SIBLING CONNECTION

As a young girl, I was troubled by speech impediments, including a slight lisp and a habit of mixing my letters. I passed this impediment to my sister as she learnt to speak, and thus, we both attended speech therapy classes. The fact speech was difficult didn't bother us at all for we had our own form of communication. I remember being fully aware of Kate's intentions and wishes long before she could speak, so words were unimportant to us. We'd look at each other, nod without saying a word, and run out to do whatever we'd decided. My poor parents found it a little freaky, but for us, it seemed perfectly normal.

Kate was born prematurely and remained in hospital for some weeks before she became strong enough to come home. I remember seeing this tiny baby with almost see-through skin and thinking, *she's mine and I will look after her.* I was only two years old, and the moment was so momentous, it forms my earliest memory. From her birth, we've been incredibly close, and that continues to this day. It was logical to me that I needed to understand this precious little thing, and I believe the wish to connect opened a form of communication that most of us have forgotten. That subconscious link that birds and fish use to move seamlessly in flocks and shoals. We accessed it because we didn't know we couldn't. We were young and without words, so we opened another, different channel.

Throughout our childhood, we had a party trick we'd roll out to impress people. One of us would stare at a playing card, and the other would have to focus and see the card using just our mental link. Over and over again, we succeeded. We were frighteningly accurate. The card would pop into my mind when she focused on it and vice versa. There was no sleight of hand or trick. We didn't need one as we'd been using this skill most of our lives.

I still get an uneasy feeling if she's upset or hurt. Invariably, when I call her, it's obvious the radio channel's still tuned in. The signal is much weaker, but in moments of need, it blares out strongly.

One day, science will uncover our ability to communicate using just the mind, but until then, society classifies our experience as paranormal - outside the normal. Consider, if you will, not so long ago, voices coming from a box, moving pictures, and talking to someone on the other side of the world would have been considered witchcraft. Things change...

3

THE LITTLE OLD LADY

I had a blessed childhood. My parents chose to leave London and raise my sister and I in the country - a decision for which I shall always be thankful.

At the age of seven, we moved onto the estate of one of England's greatest stately homes. It's a gem of the Elizabethan era set in the beautiful countryside of Wiltshire. Longleat boasts landscape gardens by Capability Brown and an art collection containing some of the world's greatest artists, such as Titian, and a couple of lesser-known artists like Hitler and Churchill.

But for a child, the more recent additions grabbed all the attention. These included the first safari park opened outside of Africa and a plethora of tourist attractions including Pet's Corner and the world's largest maze. What an amazing playground to have as a child. We ran wild, free, and happy with assorted animals and an entire estate of workers as guardians and babysitters.

But as I grew older, the very isolation I loved chafed. It was restrictive.

After much begging, bribing, and copious temper

tantrums when I was around twelve years old, my parents gave my sister and I permission to go shopping in our local town using our village bus service. I remember feeling terribly mature waiting in the little bus shelter with the ladies of the village, our fare money hot and sticky in my sweaty little hand as I waited to board the bus. I felt like an adult. I had to look after my younger sister, and I was off on a huge adventure. I seemed invincible.

Unbeknownst to me, all the women on the bus knew my parents and would keep an eye on us. My freedom was less far-reaching than I realised at the time, but still, it was a heady feeling. We boarded the bus, which meandered through the country lanes and villages, picking up the isolated villagers until it deposited us in the small market town of Frome on the Wiltshire and Somerset border. We felt so grown-up with pocket money in our purses and shops in which to spend it.

There was one particular shop on the outskirts of the town centre that we loved (for the life of me, I can't remember what the shop sold), and it was a regular stop-off point. Tall walls bordered the lane on both sides, and it ended with two rows of terrace cottages facing each other. It was a pedestrian lane, and the only openings into it were the doors from the houses. Otherwise, you'd need to walk the length of the lane to get out.

On the day in question, we were walking and chatting away, not paying particular attention to our surroundings. We'd reached the beginning of the lane and had walls on either side of us. I looked from the empty path to my sister to acknowledge something she'd said and then back - just a flick of the eyes. There in front of us stood a little old lady dressed in a dark, sombre skirt that touched her ankles, with highly polished and buttoned ankle boots. I remember they reminded me of witches' boots. Over this, she wore a long, dark, heavy tweed coat and her hair in a bun under an old-fashioned hat. She reminded me of pictures I've seen of women in the 1930s.

She appeared to be studying us both intently and, with a smile, asked after my parents and grandparents. I felt my heart race. She seemed rather sweet, but the impossibility of her appearance alarmed me. I'd only glanced away from the path for an instant, and there had been no one in the lane. I was sure because we had a clear line of vision until the very end.

My sister and I looked to each other, each wondering from where she'd appeared. We would have seen her had she opened one of the cottage doors and walk down towards us, and a woman of her age couldn't have leapt over a six-foot-high wall, so there was no obvious way she could suddenly be in front of us.

Being the eldest, I answered her questions hesitantly, telling her my parents were fine. It seemed improbable that she knew my grandparents because we'd moved down to Wiltshire, leaving my extended family in London. No one in the locality knew my grandparents, and yet, she'd asked after them with their given names. She seemed to know them, which confused us. She quizzed us a little more about them, and we answered politely.

I shot a questioning glance at my sister, and when I looked back, the woman was gone. Not a trace remained. She'd vanished in a microsecond.

This woman had appeared as solid and as real as my sister. She'd looked just like any other person walking down the street on that day, yet it made no sense. My sister and I were both frightened and sprinted up the street to the shop.

We agreed we'd take the long route back and avoid the lane on the way home.

A few months later, I visited my grandmother in London and mentioned the little old lady who'd been asking after her. My grandmother asked me to describe the woman, which I did. She smiled at me and asked me to wait a moment whilst she retrieved something. After rummaging, she pulled out an aged, tired, black-and-white photo of the little woman we'd seen in the street.

"That's her, Nanny. That's the lady we saw." I was so excited because I realised that this woman was known to my family.

My grandmother smiled and proceeded to tell me a story so improbable, it blew my mind. She told me the lady in the lane was my great-grandmother, a woman who'd died many years before, when my father was just a small boy. I couldn't believe my ears or my eyes. How had I met the woman if she'd been dead for thirty-five years?

My grandmother told me about my great-grandmother, her mother-in-law. She said if anybody would keep an eye on the family and make certain we were well, it would be my great-grandmother. It seemed my sister and I weren't the first members of the family she'd paid a visit to. In my grandmother's house, my aunts, father, and even my mother were each woken by a woman at the end of the bed watching over them. It seemed my great-grandmother kept an eye on our entire family.

I've never seen Grandma Uffelmann again. I've never even dreamt of her, but it warms my heart to think she keeps an eye on us from a distance. What is clear is that on that day, when I was twelve, I was lucky enough to meet my long-dead great-grandmother.

4

GUILT EASED

When I was twelve years old, I moved from a tiny village school with only thirty students to a secondary school with over 1,500. My primary school held the children of our small village, many of whose families had lived there for generations. Everyone knew everyone else, and the children were sheltered.

The secondary school was in a military garrison town housing the families of the soldiers who worked on Salisbury Plain - one of the UK's largest military zones. The army barracks were like a small town in their own right, and the houses saw an ever-changing stream of families. A single classroom in my new school held more pupils than the entire student body of my primary school. It was intimidating for a shy introvert such as me.

Only three children moved up from my primary school that year. The school put two of them together in a class. I wasn't so lucky. I found myself alone in a new class with thirty strangers. It was terrifying.

There was one girl though, bouncy and full of life, who stood out. She approached me and chatted away happily despite just receiving shy nods from me. She didn't care I was shy. She had enough verve for both of us, and we soon became firm friends. Her parents had arrived with the military and chosen to stay when her father joined civvy street. Not only did she like me but she would not be moving on when the garrisons changed. I'd won the friendship lottery.

Soon we organised stay-overs and dinners at each other's houses. Her parents were Welsh, and I loved their lilting tones (they were my first exposure to the Welsh accent). She also had two younger sisters who enchanted me. We were building the foundations of a great friendship, and her exuberance boosted my confidence, helping me to come out of my shell.

One summer evening, I was having supper at her house, and my parents were due to pick me up later in the evening. We enjoyed our time laughing, whispering secrets, and planning our next adventure.

Anyone who knows me will tell you I have a notoriously bad relationship with time. I don't believe in the concept of time, and I hold it in little regard. This was a feature I shared with my parents, so I've always found myself late everywhere. Even if I try to be on time, leaving plenty of time to get ready, when I next check a clock, I'm already seriously late. Time flows differently for me.

On this occasion, I'd agreed to meet my parents some distance from my friend's house. She'd generously offered to walk with me to the meeting place, so we'd set off with her sisters in tow. We cut the journey by taking a shortcut down a local bridle-path and chatted whilst we waited for them. As always, we waited a long time as they were late. I said my farewell, belted myself into the car, and went home unaware that night would be the last night of our friendship.

The next day, I got the heart wrenching news that on the

walk home, my friend's little sister, Marsha, had been killed. A horse box travelling too fast along the path and blinded by the setting sun had struck her, killing her instantly.

It was the first real death I'd ever dealt with. I'd seen many dead animals and even handled them, but I'd never been close to a tragic death like this. I felt I'd been filleted, as if my guts were on display to the world. How could that gorgeous little girl, only about seven years old, no longer be with us? I blamed myself. If my parents hadn't been late, she wouldn't have been on that road and would still be alive. I'd killed her. Now, looking back with the lens of an adult, I can see that is blatantly untrue, but as a fragile young twelve-year-old, I believed I was to blame.

When my friend returned to school, she'd changed. The sunshine had gone. It was as if the death had tarnished her. To this day, I don't know if my guilt put a barrier between us or if her own pain associated me with the event, but our friendship faded and died. Her golden glow never returned. I would see her around the school in the years that followed, but our friendship never recovered.

Years later, when I passed my driving test, I drove to the graveyard to visit Marsha's grave. I'd never gone before, but I felt the need to see it and apologise for my involvement in her death. I laid down flowers, cried, and apologised. It was poignant and cathartic. After this, I didn't consciously think much more about the event.

One day, when I was around twenty-two, I left work and drove home in my shiny red Sierra, not thinking about anything much except supper and bed. As I pulled into the parking bay, I looked up at my house, and there at the front door, smiling sweetly, was Marsha, just as I'd last seen her. She watched me silently for some moments before nodding at me with a huge smile and fading away. I remember screeching in shock and then being sure my work stress was affecting me. With time, I persuaded myself it was all in my imagination.

Another six months passed with no further sightings, and I relaxed. One evening, I was watching TV with my boyfriend, and suddenly, there she was again, in the gap behind the TV. She nodded again, smiled, and faded away. I told my boyfriend, who swore he hadn't seen a thing. I became unsettled. After over ten years, why was this happening? Was it some form of repressed stress brought out by my workload? I knew I'd pushed my feelings down all those years before, but I didn't understand why they were coming to the fore now.

The final episode happened when I was in bed one night. I was reading, and I looked up to turn the side lamp off, and there she was again, standing by my bedroom door, watching me. She nodded, she smiled, and she faded.

From that day on, I never saw her again.

Eight years later, I attended a reading with a famous local psychic as a favour for my friend who wanted to go. She booked the appointment in her name for two people. I was an utter sceptic and wanted to give the man no opportunity to investigate me and con me with his clever research, which is what I believed psychics did.

When it came time for me to meet the man, I was presented with the cutest little grandpa of a man you could ever hope to meet. I couldn't believe such a man would lie, but that was probably how he lured people into trusting him, I reasoned. I sat down with my ankles crossed and hands folded as if in prayer. I refused to meet his eyes as I didn't want my body language to give him clues.

His opening statement cut me to the core. "Who is Marsha? I have her here. She wants you to know it was her time to go, and you are not to blame. You never were. She tells me she visited you three times to show you she was okay, but you rejected her. Marsha wants you to know she's fine, and you need to let her go, so she can move along her path."

Tears were pouring down my face. There was no way he could have known this. I was no longer in contact with any of my school friends, and no one else knew of this event. I hadn't mentioned it to any of my new friends. Yet, he knew her name. He knew I'd seen her three times and that I carried a bone-aching guilt.

He carried on to tell me many frighteningly accurate details about other aspects of my life, even mentioning that I shared his gift should I wish to explore it, but it was his opening words that left me leaving that room free of guilt for the first time in eighteen years. After that, I could remember Marsha, the girl, rather than just her death. With time, her impact on my life has lessened, although she will always hold a place in my heart.

5

FINAL FAREWELL

Sometimes you say a casual farewell to someone before hopping on a plane, car, or train, and fate denies you the chance to say goodbye again. If you'd known that would be your last farewell, you'd have handled it so differently. You'd have focused and told them how much they meant to you. You'd mark the occasion with your full being and mental presence.

Unfortunately, you rarely realise that this farewell will be your last, and most people don't get the opportunity to revisit it - but I did.

It was midsummer. I was dating a wonderful man, Mac, who was the kindest, most sincere and loving person. Every time I met someone who knew him, no matter how vaguely, they would say, "He's my best friend."

I'd never met someone with so many people who adored him, and yet, I understood why. He was so caring and thoughtful. He set reminders on his phone for the important events of everyone he knew, no matter how remotely. This was long before automated Facebook reminders made it easy, and on their special days, he called them to say happy birthday, happy anniversary, or even to acknowledge their kid's birthdays. He didn't do it for the credit but because people mattered to him.

We were living in Egypt, and there were beggars everywhere, some genuine and some career beggars. Most of the people I knew paid them little attention because if you gave to one, you'd be swarmed with an army of others. Yet, Mac didn't ignore them. He actively searched them out, even doing U-turns whilst driving if he'd spotted someone on the side of the road and couldn't pull up in time. He'd go back and give them a little money and a lot of his time.

He saw them not as a beggar but as a person, and he reached out to them and gave them something few did - the gift of acknowledging their humanity and their existence. In Egypt, like most developing countries, the destitute become invisible but never to him.

I once asked him why he gave to everyone when there were so many professional beggars. He replied, as if it were the most obvious answer in the world, "I'd rather give to all than miss the one who needs my help."

We were happy, and both of us looked to the future with joy. Then I was needed at home.

My sister, Kate, was heavily pregnant with her second child, and I'd agreed to be her birthing partner. I was excited to return to the UK to support her and meet this new little member of my family. I was distracted as we said goodbye, and I don't remember the moment at all. I'm sure we hugged and promised to speak each day. I hopped onto the plane to England without a backward glance.

When I arrived, my sister was vast (she may kill me later for writing that) and very uncomfortable. She was more than ready for the birth. As it was a scheduled caesarean, we knew when it was happening, so everything was calm. We kissed my brother-in-law and niece goodbye, and I drove Kate to her local maternity wing.

The hospital gave me unattractive green scrubs to wear in the operating theatre, and my sister broke down into such hysterics when she saw me in them that I feared she would deliver there and then. The birth proceeded well, overseen by an Egyptian surgeon. The world is an odd place - I'd flown from Egypt to England for my sister's delivery only to be chatting in Arabic in the operating room.

I witnessed my nephew's birth, heard his first little squalling cry, and was humbled by the miracle of life. I called Mac to share the news. He'd just been to the dentist and had a tooth extracted, so the conversation was one-sided, but to be honest, it would have been anyway as I was bursting with news about my gorgeous baby nephew.

Mac told me that he was taking a group for a diving trip to the famous Blue Hole, a deep and cavernous hole in the sea floor close to the coastline of the laid-back town of Darhab. I remember distinctly the overwhelming feeling of foreboding this announcement induced. He was a dive master and hosted groups most weekends, and I trusted him implicitly. He was sensible and careful, and yet, on this occasion, I wasn't happy. I remember begging him not to go so soon after having a tooth out. I thought the pressure of the dive wouldn't be good for it. Mac laughed my worries away and asked me to describe the baby.

The next day dawned, heralding the arrival of all the relatives eager to meet our chubby little fellow. I met up with my parents, and we took my eighteen-month-old niece to the beach to give my sister and brother-in-law time alone with their new son.

That night, I tried to call Mac but didn't get an answer. It was unusual, but I figured he was busy entertaining his group. I kept trying, but the phone just rang out time after time. I sent him a text which I will always remember. The words haunt me:

Do I still have a boyfriend alive out there?

The next morning, he still hadn't replied, and the silence felt ominous. My brother-in-law had gone to the hospital to see my sister and the baby. I was home alone with my tiny niece. I rang our mutual friend in Egypt to see if he'd heard from him.

"He's gone, Hazel."

"Gone where? What are you saying?"

"He died yesterday."

Until that day, I wouldn't have thought I could make the noise that left my body. It was a primeval howl. I sounded like a wounded animal. My legs collapsed, and the sound wouldn't stop. I remember little. It seems I called my sister and my best friend. Kate discharged herself from the hospital and came home, and between her and my friend, they found me transit back to Egypt. The funeral was the next day, and I needed to get back for it.

The taxi from Devon to Bath was a blur. My friend pulled me from the back of the cab into his arms and took me from Bath to Heathrow in his car. I remember flashes of the journey. I was so deeply in shock. I didn't cry as such. Water just poured unchecked down my cheeks. Inside, I was frozen.

After a four-hour journey, I'd arrived at Heathrow. My friend dropped me at departures and went to park. I made my way to check-in, and they informed me they'd overbooked the flight and denied me access. I fainted. I think my body just couldn't take any more bad news. I tried to explain the situation, how critically I needed to catch the flight, but the ground staff were unyielding. My friend arrived and took over, and I found myself on a flight to Frankfurt. From there, I was to fly to Stockholm and spend a night in a hotel and then, in the morning, fly on to Cairo. I honestly remember nothing of the flight to, arrival at, or departure from Frankfurt, nor the arrival at Stockholm.

It's an odd sensation to be in Heathrow one moment and find yourself alone in a super modern, white Scandinavian hotel room the next. Yet, that is exactly how it seemed to me. I was colder than I'd ever been. It was the middle of July, so far from cold, and yet, I felt as if I was carved from a block of glacial ice. I felt just as fragile.

Shivers wracked me, so I took a hot shower to warm up. It was the first time I'd been on my own since the news broke, and my barriers collapsed in that shower. I cried like I've never cried, and I mourned. I mourned him. I mourned us. I mourned the future that would never be. And somehow, I slowly warmed up, and a calmness descended.

I wrapped myself in one of the thick, fluffy white robes that the hotel supplied, wrapped a towel around my head, and stood by the mirror just staring at myself. All I could see was a haunted girl lost behind the puffy eyes and white skin. It was me, and yet, I was lost somewhere in my body. And then…

Warm arms wrapped around me from behind, crossing my chest and gripping my arms in a huge, warm, and totally comforting hug. His aftershave engulfed me, and I felt a firm and loving kiss on my cheek. I closed my eyes and luxuriated in the embrace. I felt love radiating towards me and a calm, clear acceptance.

The hug eased, and I heard, "Goodbye, Hazy." The scent floated away, and he was gone.

From that moment forward, I was calm. I knew he was okay. I grieved and mourned and hurt but with a different level of acceptance. I didn't rail against God and destiny as so many of our friends and loved ones did because I knew without a shadow of doubt that he was okay. He was gone from this plane, but he was okay.

When I arrived in Cairo, I was picked up by mutual friends and taken to my apartment. They explained that Mac had been on a standard dive with a handful of other divers. One of the less experienced in the group panicked and grabbed onto Mac's friend, Sami, another Dive Master. The combined weight made them plummet to dangerous depths. Mac followed and managed to get the panic-crazed man off Sami.

He gestured, in dive signs, that Sami should return to the surface and get help, and he'd stay to keep the man calm. The man, by this time crazed with decompression toxicity, latched onto Mac, and they dropped out of sight in seconds. Sami dived down to dangerous levels, desperate to find them, but with no success. They both died that day.

I later learnt that Sami had returned to their room after the search party was cancelled for the evening, opened Mac's phone to call me, and saw my message. I never saw or heard from him again – I think it was too raw for both of us.

In an odd twist of fate, I'd nearly drowned two years previously. The memory of the sense of complete tranquillity that had overcome me just before I passed out gave me such comfort when dealing with Mac's death.

Mac died saving his friend and trying to help a terrified man. That, more than anything, signifies the type of man he was.

I'd arrived in Cairo two hours too late for his funeral. So, instead, for about two months, I visited his tomb nearly every day, always hoping he'd return and spend more time with me.

He never did.

He'd said his goodbye that evening in Stockholm, and he'd given me a gift many people don't get when their loved ones are killed in a tragic accident: the gift of acceptance and, of course, the chance for a final farewell.

6
THE WARNING

My career has taken me all around the world. My home was wherever I placed my suitcase. So, I valued the time I could spend in the UK.

For a while, both my sister and I lived in Bath, a world heritage city clothed in the golden hues of the local stone, famous for its elegant Georgian crescents and Jane Austen stories. When my sister married and started having children, she moved away to Devon, a county bordered by the English Channel and the Atlantic Ocean, much lauded for its bucolic scenery, from green rolling fields to haunting empty moors.

After the desert scrub-land of Egypt, I longed for the green lands of England. Whenever I flew home, I would divide my time between my flat in Bath and my sister's house in Devon.

On this occasion, I was returning to Bath after spending a lovely weekend with my sister and her family. I'd left a little later than I preferred, finding it hard to tear myself away from my young niece and nephew, and the sun was hanging low in the sky. I was driving along a stretch of road called the A380, which cuts through heavy forests and scrubby heathland. It's notoriously dangerous, a dual carriageway that sweeps down mighty hills and sloping bends, the scene of many fatalities.

That evening, I was in a mellow mood, driving along in a daydream, allowing my subconscious mind to drive the car along this familiar path. I had a two-hour journey in front of me, mostly along boring motorways, so I decided to put on some music. I looked down to the stereo to select the radio channel.

Then a voice screamed at me, "SLOW DOWN!"

I slammed the brakes on and looked up to see a huge stag jump free of the dense woodland, into the path of my vehicle. My car slid, losing its traction on the road, and all I could see was it heading toward the majestic deer. Just as I'd decided my fate had been sealed, the tyres found traction. The car slowed, missing the deer by just a few centimetres.

My heart was jumping out of my chest as I struggled to understand what had just happened. Shaken by the experience, I pulled over into a lay-by to gather my nerves before continuing the journey.

I'd heard that voice so clearly, so strongly, and it had literally saved my life. Yet, there was no one except me in the car. Sometimes you can hear your own thoughts. This wasn't that. This was a clear male voice that saved my life and that of the deer. Without his warning, I wouldn't have seen the deer until too late and would have hit it at seventy miles per hour. I can't say I would've died, but I know without doubt I would have at least been horribly injured.

I can't tell you whose voice that was, nor can I say I recognised the voice because I didn't. What I can say is that whoever it was had been watching over me. He warned me before the deer had even leapt from the forest. I'd never been much of a believer in guardian angels, a concept hijacked by hippies and tree-huggers, yet from that day forward, I've believed someone watches over us.

I'm afraid I've given my poor guardian rather more work than he deserves. So far, I suspect he's had a hand in saving me from a car crash, three near drownings, and a potentially deadly bout of gangrene. I owe him my thanks.

7

FIREFLIES

After Mac died, I continued on in Egypt, struggling to come to terms with his death. Our closest friend, Mohamed, was also struggling, and that battle to come to terms with our mutual tragedy created a tight bond. He patiently helped me to overcome endless issues, not least a crushing water phobia that sprung up after Mac's death.

We nursed each other through the dark days, and with time, our friendship blossomed into something more. Somehow, I knew that Mac would've blessed our union, so after a few years, Mohamed and I married.

I moved into Mohamed's large villa on a ranch in rural Egypt. Lush farmland between the Great Pyramids of Giza and the Saqqara Step Pyramid surrounded us. From the flat roof of my house, I could see both sets of pyramids, so although I was in the middle of the tourist zone, we were miles outside the hustle and bustle of Cairo.

Unless you live in the country, you will never appreciate how dark night can be without the orange glow of streetlights. In the middle of the farming land, we didn't suffer from light pollution, especially as our rooms had industrial-strength blackout curtains. At night, the darkness was absolute and accompanied by utter silence, except for the haunting shriek of the Karawan (a night bird) or the ritual calls to prayer from the local mosque.

One evening in early 2007, we'd enjoyed a pleasant but ordinary evening. Mohamed and I'd shared a light supper and moved furniture around in his office to make room for an antique sideboard. It had belonged to his grandmother and was full of her old possessions. We'd spent the afternoon going through the old letters and photos that shone such light on her personality. We'd retired to bed, and I was reading by the gentle glow of my Kindle whilst Mohamed slept next to me. I'm an ardent reader and always read in bed, but to not disturb my husband, I turn the Kindle's light to its lowest setting.

I was reading, lost in the world of fiction, when a mass of little blue sparks, like fireflies, started to fly around our bed. They whirled and swooped, like swallows in the sky, playing around Mohamed's body and head. I watched in astonishment, frozen in disbelief, yet enchanted by the almost fairy-like display. I remember shaking my head to clear my eyes, sure they were playing a trick on me. Maybe I was so tired that I was seeing things.

Then, from nowhere, I was overwhelmed with a feeling of such deep love and adoration. It was as if a fire of the purest and vastest love had overtaken my body. I was receiving, like a radio, someone else's feelings. It wasn't my emotion but an emotion being played to me. Somehow, I knew this energy was visiting Mohamed and loved him deeply. I still can't put into words how I knew this. It was as if the knowledge arrived fully formed and certain.

I whispered his name, careful not to disturb the little

sparks of energy, and shook his shoulder. He grumbled, waking slowly, asking me why I'd woken him. I described what I was seeing and ask him if he saw anything. He didn't. He asked me to narrate what I was witnessing in real time, which I did.

For over twenty minutes I lay watching the display that reminded me of a murmuration of starlings, twirling and whirling around him. The sparks seemed to flow through the shades of blue, from deep sapphire to the palest baby blue, but the dominating colour was the vibrant azure of the Mediterranean. Sometimes, wisps of the cluster would stretch out towards me, but the bulk swept the planes of his body, always about a foot above him, almost as if they were playing with him. If he lifted his arm, the sparks moved with the arm, caressing it from a distance before flitting away.

Throughout the entire time I was bathed in this beautiful, warm glow of love, which was both deeply moving and poignant. Then, slowly, one by one, each of the sparks faded away, and the emotions lessened until we were left in the dark and empty room.

We chatted about the experience in wonder and awe, astounded to have experienced such a bizarre, yet strangely beautiful phenomena. I guess I'm lucky that Mohamed believed me and didn't call a doctor to have me checked over. Both of us, to this day, believe unlocking his grandmother's sideboard encouraged her to visit us that night. I wish I'd met her in life. She's always been described in such loving terms, but I feel I was lucky enough to experience the warmth of her love that night.

It wasn't a solitary experience. For some time after that evening, both Mohamed and I saw the gorgeous energy sparks return but never with the same intensity or strength.

I will always feel I was truly blessed that night.

8

THE SCENTS

For as long as I can remember, I've smelt phantom scents. Scents that appear from nowhere linger for a moment before disappearing without a trace. Mostly, they materialise when I'm alone, reading or watching TV, when I'm not focused or thinking about anything. They coalesce and are overwhelmingly strong, as if someone just sprayed perfume into my face. Often, the scents are old-fashioned floral perfumes, and sometimes, although rarely, they are more masculine.

In my husband Mohamed's villa, which he'd built surrounded by farmland outside Cairo, I would sit alone on my sofa and be overwhelmed with the heady aroma of old English roses. It's such an evocative scent and seldomly used anymore, yet it would surround me on that sofa. We didn't have any roses in the house, nor in the garden, and we didn't use rose-scented cleaning or air-freshening products. Yet, night after night, it would envelope me. Mohamed never detected it and was sceptical that I did, so after a while, I stopped mentioning it.

A couple of years after moving into the house, my sister came to visit. She asked me about the gorgeous rose scent in the house. I was excited that someone else had at last experienced it, and when I quizzed her, she confirmed she only smelt it whilst sitting alone on that one sofa. I asked around my family and Mohamed's family to see if any of our close relatives had ever worn a heavy rose perfume and came back with a blank.

Until my last day in that house, the beautiful floral scent of old English roses often visited me.

I began to wonder about this peculiar phenomenon. Why did I smell things no one else could? I'd smelt Mac's aftershave when he came to say farewell. I'd be alone and suddenly wrapped in the essence of *L'aiment,* a perfume my beloved and long-gone grandmother wore. I'd be walking my dog and suddenly have exotic floral perfume all around me when walking down a lonely country lane. Why?

Being a business consultant, I was well used to research, so I began to dig into the subject. One potential cause could be a brain tumour. I quickly discounted this because I'd been experiencing it since childhood, and at that point, I was in my late thirties. Then I came across a fascinating article on clairalience (the ability for a person to acquire psychic knowledge by means of smelling). This seemed to encapsulate what I'd been experiencing all my life.

It still happens to me frequently. Just the other day, I was in a tyre repair centre with my father. We were sat in the waiting room on our own, and suddenly I smelt the most powerful, heavy, spicy aftershave. I moved around the waiting room, and the scent was limited to the chair next to mine. As soon as I moved away from that chair, the smell vanished. When I returned, the cheap aftershave was as powerful as ever. My father smelt nothing.

Vapours

It's not a particularly impressive paranormal skill, but as I come across it so often it's probably my strongest.

9

PSYCHICS AND ME

I have mixed feelings about psychics. As I mentioned earlier in *Guilt Eased,* my first ever visit to a psychic was earth-shattering. The details he knew were impossible to guess or research. However, I believe there are charlatans who ride the coattails of people's anguish and grief, separating them from their money with psychological tricks and advanced body reading skills. I have come across these people in my travels, and I abhor them. They are profiteering from the pain of others, and that's just plain wrong.

I try to avoid psychics. I've seen enough to know there is more to life than we see, and I don't feel comfortable exploring that beyond the natural circumstances I come across. However, both my sister and father are fascinated with the spiritual world, and they've dragged me, screaming and shouting, along to various spiritual churches, psychic readings, and private sessions. On every occasion, the psychic swoops down on me and shares details of my life with the enthralled audience, from my stubborn nature (true, unfortunately) to marital disagreements to health issues and the names of people I've lost.

Perhaps they were lucky guesses, or the psychic had researched my background. Yet, on every occasion I've attended, at the last minute, without sharing my name or any details with the psychic or the organiser, they were able to capture totally accurate details about me.

I've had four psychics tell me I'm a writer. During a period of profound self-doubt, when I'd stopped writing for over two years, one told me it was my destiny to write and I needed to stop doubting myself and write again, not for me but for my readers. Now writing isn't a trade that leaves clear markers, like working in a fish and chip shop could leave a scent or building could create tanned skin and calloused hands. Maybe in the times of Dickens, writers could be identified by ink-smeared hands but not anymore. How could they know I'm a writer?

I've heard psychics saying, "I have an 'M' here. Does that mean anything to any of you? No? Oh, maybe it's an 'N'." I call that out as pure blarney. They're fishing, throwing out bait to lure in a target. In my case, psychics have turned to me saying, "I have Marsha here," or "I have Caroline here - how you loved to dance together, then go back to her flat and read until the sun rose." They are always specific and correct.

Perhaps the most shockingly accurate reading came from a psychic who called out my dog's extraordinary name. Mohamed and I inherited the dog from his cousin. It was called Hitler. In Egypt, it's common practise to name a dog after something awful, like Satan or Hitler, etc. to keep the "Evil Eye" away from the home. Nevertheless, I couldn't cope, as a British woman, with having a dog in the house called Hitler. He was a gorgeous black Great Dane and utterly lovable, so we tried to change his name to Hunter but to no avail. So, we ended up with a dog called Hitler.

In the UK, no one would ever call a dog by that reviled name, and rightly so. Yet, in another session, a world-renowned psychic called out just that. He said he had a dog with a military leader's name and then, in hushed disbelief, said, "Hitler. The dog's name is Hitler?" That was embarrassing, admitting it was me and having to explain why.

On many occasions, I've received messages for people I know, every time in acute detail and accuracy. I was asked to help my friend's family accept her early demise from cancer and to pass on regards to my in-laws from my husband's grandfather.

The more they focus on me, the more I try to avoid such events. Until recently, when, aghast that I was once again the centre of attention, I asked the psychic afterwards why I was receiving such clear and detailed readings from members of his profession. He was a sweet, slightly elderly man, and he smiled and said, "My dear, you are a receiver, open to the spirits, so you amplify their energy and make it easy for people such as I to have a clear and open channel with the spirits interested in you."

When I shared this with my mother later, she reminded me of my first visit to the psychic who'd told me about Marsha. He'd told me all those years ago that I shared his gift, but I refused to accept it. He told me if I wanted to develop it, I could as I had a strong latent talent. I didn't want to then, I don't now, and I never will. But maybe it's that "gift", for want of a better word, that shines a spotlight over my head at these events.

I still feel uncomfortable around psychics. Far too many have taken on the rock star status of celebrity. But the humble few who truly bear the gift of the sight, in my experience, are the ones who give from their heart and don't need staging. I feel for them because as much as it's a gift, it's also a curse. My first psychic was in the army, and before a battle, he would see spirits gathering around his comrades who wouldn't survive. Some spirits who couldn't communicate verbally instead shared their pain with him. It's not something I'd ever want to experience or explore, but as a writer, it opens questions.

What if you were a nurse and could see which of the patients would die that day?

What if you were a writer but found your muse was telling you the life stories of the spirits around you?

What lengths would you go to as a psychic to stop a person's death you'd foreseen?

These are the questions that form the shiny nugget of a new story from which authors find inspiration.

10

THE INFLUENCING FACTOR

I've shared my paranormal experiences, but what impact did they have on my writing?

I suspect every writer's journey of inspiration is different. If I polled writers on this, there would be as many forms of inspiration as writers themselves. News stories to life events, daydreams to nightmares – they are all forms of inspiration.

For me, it all started with a dream. One day, I was rudely awakened from a fascinating dream. It was set in Egypt, and I was about 75% of the way through it when my well-meaning husband woke me with a cup of coffee. Normally, that would be a great start to the morning, but I was furious. What happened? How did the story end? So, my novel was literally delivered into my sleeping head, gift-wrapped with a big bow.

I'd always wanted to be a writer, but my high-pressured career left little time for life, let alone writing. Most days, I worked twelve hours, grabbed a sandwich, and flopped into bed, only to start the same cycle the next day. It was brutal.

This dream coincided with a period of severe health

issues that put the kibosh on my consulting career, so I found myself homebound with nothing to do. I decided if I wanted to know the end of the story, then I'd better write it, and for five years, that is what I did. Like a sculptor, I had the rough block of stone. I knew what the end item should look like, and I chipped away until the stone revealed the core of the item.

That story became *House of Scarabs*, the first in my series, and spawned *Genesis* and my next project, *House of Bastet*. It was a story of three perfectly normal people who'd, unbeknownst to them, had been committed to a cause by their ancestors generations ago. What I loved about the story was the concept of what happens if good people have potentially bad powers. What if the heroes of the story are actually the villains, and the villains were fighting for the sake of good? That fascinated me. But giving no spoilers, for those of you who've yet to read *House of Scarabs*, it was the paranormal focus that captured my imagination. The concept of what happens after life and what if life could continue after death? Without all my own experiences, I doubt I would have that innate curiosity about the thin veil between life and death.

Since I started writing, I've found the ideas for books often come to me well-formed in dreams. That was the case with a new comedic series I'll start after *House of Bastet*. It's about a shy young woman, overpowered and bullied by her domineering mother, who isn't released from her influence even after the mother's death.

Sometimes, daydreams create the gem of an idea, as was the case with the *Land of Clouds*. With that story, I was flying from England to Egypt, staring out the window. I saw the clouds as a landscape and imagined a spirit race that lived in the clouds. That story is now on my writing radar.

What links all these stories is the otherworldly essence of the paranormal. I am fascinated with what could be out there just beyond our senses. The life-after-death or life on other planes. These are the stories that I want to explore.

There is only one book I want to write outside this sphere, and that's a deeply personal and political piece that I don't feel I've the writing muscles to attack yet. I hope I get the chance one day because the story is hugely meaningful to me.

Would I still carry this fascination with the paranormal if I hadn't had such powerful experiences myself? Who knows? All I can say with certainty is that they've added fuel to the desire to understand more and explore possibilities - albeit via the written word.

11

IN CLOSING

As is so often the case for writers, by committing these encounters to paper, I've learnt (or learned, depending which side of the pond you're on) so much about myself. I started this project because I thought it would be an interesting thing to share with my readers, but I've ended it seeing myself through a new lens.

The calm level of acceptance I've always had when faced with these abnormal situations makes me think I've always been more closely linked to the veil than I'd previously believed. As I was writing the stories and getting feedback from my family, they reminded me of so many other, more minor, experiences we or I'd faced. It became apparent that my family is inherently more open to the unexplainable than most.

My grandmother saved my aunt's life by following her intuition. Her panicked call notified people of the potentially deadly brain haemorrhage that had left my aunt dysfunctional and unable to call for help. Yet, my grandmother was miles away and hadn't seen or spoken to my aunt.

I now believe some of us still use the oldest of senses, the ones that animals use to communicate or to sense danger. It's possible our primitive brain is still more active than most people's. Who knows? I am positive that someday, science will explain the inexplicable, and everything I've experienced will be understood without fear, mockery, or contempt.

There is more to this world than we understand, and I will continue to explore that theme, as I have in *House of Scarabs* and *Genesis*, to process my experiences and ask, **"What if?"**

> *What if life continues after death?*
> *What if your soul could be reincarnated?*
> *What if our life is just a part of the soul's learning*
>   *phase before it metamorphoses into*
> *something more?*
> *What if your guardian angel was just an*
>   *instructor keeping an eye on your soul?*

"What if..." is the source of all stories and where I shall leave you.

I hope we meet again someday between the pages of another book.

HOUSE OF SCARABS

Three strangers are bound together by ancient Egyptian prophecy. Will they survive long enough to uncover what the gods have in store?

Ellie has been betrayed by everyone she's ever met. Still recovering from her ex-husband's infidelity and the death of her unborn child, she throws herself into teaching Arabic classes. Not even her charismatic new student, Ben, can break through the defenses surrounding her heart. But a fateful trip to a bookstore specializing in ancient mythology will force the polar opposites to work together in a divine mission beyond their wildest imaginations…

Gerhard strives to be a pillar of his tight-knit community. As the owner of a bookshop devoted to mythology, the widower hopes to share the treasures of antiquity with future generations. When Gerhard, Ben, and Ellie cross paths among the stacks of books, a primeval force bonds the three of them together. Confused and unprepared for a mythical quest, they're sent on a dangerous mission that will take them from pastoral England to the shifting dunes of Egypt…

When an archaic order of assassins aims to stop them at any cost, Ellie, Ben, and Gerhard must quickly uncover their connection to the Egyptian gods. If they fail their mission, then their inexplicably connected lives may be lost in the sands of time…

House of Scarabs is the first book in *The House of Scarabs* action-thriller series. If you like quirky characters, tales of mysterious ancient powers, and fast-paced action in exotic locales, then you'll love Hazel Longuet's enthralling novel!

Visit www.hazellonguet.com to learn more about *House of Scarabs* and unravel the mystery of the gods today!

GENESIS

Faced with the extinction of their faith, the high priest of Egypt must take steps to preserve the gods' knowledge for the sake of the pharaoh's immortality.

One vision rocks the foundations of the Egyptian belief system. The pharaoh's seer knows that their civilisation will perish and their faith fall fallow. Horrified at the implication, she shares the news with the high priest of Egypt. Only together can they plant a seed that will allow the culture to return and flourish. Her vision is clear. They must select a group of men who will carry the power of the ancient gods in their blood. They will form a secret organisation that will cross the plains and oceans to ensure that one day, the pharaohs can rise again and reclaim their rightful place as world leaders.

Nothing must stop them - not even the pharaoh.

The only problem is they have a spy in their midst who will stop at nothing to ensure they fail.

Genesis is the prequel to *House of Scarabs* and should ideally be read after it. If you like historical thrillers, quirky characters, and tales of mysterious ancient powers, then you'll love this novella.

Visit www.hazellonguet.com to learn more.

AFTERWORD

Thank You

Yay! You made it all the way to the end. **Thank you** for the time you've shared with me whilst reading my book. I hope you've taken something away from the experience, if only a few moments of escapism from the rigours of the everyday world.

As a member of my email community, you will get a regular newsletter about my writing adventures as well as exclusive

Afterword

reader perks. These will only be limited by my imagination and will include: short stories, keys to unlock secret online adventures, videos, sneak previews of new books, and the chance to join my advanced team. If you enjoyed reading this book, you'll love the things I share in the community. To join visit my website at www.hazellonguet.com.

Advance Team

If you'd like to get your hands on my books first, for free, in exchange for an impartial review on Amazon, Goodreads or Bookbub, visit www.hazellonguet.com/arclp and join my Advanced Team.

Critique Team

If you'd like to play a more involved role in the creation of my books, I have a select number of readers who get my first draft, before any editing or primping. These readers help me identify issues with the book and tell me areas they'd like expanded or reduced, if the characters are working and fully formed, etc. If you'd like to join my Critique Team, I'd love to have you. You can join by visiting www.hazellonguet.com/betalp and signing up.

How to Contact Me

When my characters haven't taken me hostage, dragging me into the world of their stories, you can find me hanging out in the following places:

Facebook: Go to www.facebook.com/HazelLonguetAuthor and follow my Facebook Page

Afterword

TikTok: Go to www.tiktok.com/HazelLonguetAuthor to follow me.

Email: If you'd like to drop me a line, please do so at **hlonguet@hazellonguet.com**. I love to read the emails, and I try to respond wherever possible.

Printed in Great Britain
by Amazon